DISCOVERING SACRED TEXTS

Series editor:
W. Owen Cole

Buddhist Scriptures

Anil Goonewardene

HEINEMANN

Heinemann Library
an imprint of Heinemann Publishers (Oxford) Ltd
Halley Court, Jordan Hill, Oxford OX2 8EJ

OXFORD LONDON EDINBURGH MADRID
ATHENS BOLOGNA PARIS MELBOURNE
SYDNEY AUCKLAND SINGAPORE
TOKYO IBADAN NAIROBI HARARE
GABORONE PORTSMOUTH NH (USA)

A catalogue record for this book is available from the British Library

ISBN 0 431 07375 9
98 97 96 95 94
10 9 8 7 6 5 4 3 2 1

Designed and produced by Visual Image, Street
Cover design by Philip Parkhouse, Abingdon
Produced by Mandarin Offset
Printed and bound in Hong Kong

Introduction to the series

The purpose of these books is to show what the scriptures of the six religions in the series are, to tell the story of how they grew into their present form, and to give some idea of how they are used and what they mean to believers. It is hoped that readers will be able to appreciate how important the sacred texts are to those who base their lives on them and use them to develop their faith as well as their knowledge. For this reason, members of the six major religions found in Britain today have been asked to write these books.

W. Owen Cole (Series Editor)

Dedication

This book is dedicated with love and respect to my parents. May they attain Nibbana.

Acknowledgements

I thank everyone who has helped me in the work for this book. Special thanks to Professor Richard Gombrich, Brian Netto and Ven. Pandit Dr Medagama Vajiragnana for advice on the structure of the book, to Ven. Myokyo-ni and Malcolm Songest for commenting on some units, to Ganshin Rock for information on Buddhism in Japan and to Professor Lakshman Perera for help at every stage of the work and for commenting on each of the units. Similarly, thanks to Owen Cole, Sue Walton, Tristan Boyer and Alison Sims for their editorial work and for their kindness about my delays in doing the work, and finally to my wife Sunethra for her encouragement, advice and help. Some faults will remain; they are mine alone. I hope that users of this book will point them out to me.

The Publishers would like to thank the following for permission to reproduce photographs: The British Library pp. 13, 23; The British Museum pp. 24, 25; Dr D. K. Goonewardene pp. 8, 9; Graham Harrison pp. 7, 15, 17, 19, 44, 45, 46; 'Green Khadiravani Tara', central regions, Tibet, circa first half of twelfth century, Tangra, gouache on cotton, Mr and Mrs John Gilmore Fund/Royal Academy of Arts p. 38; The Hutchison Library p. 14; Mrs Reiko Rock p. 42; The Royal Academy of Arts p. 29; Zefa Picture Library p. 36.

The Publishers would like to thank Robin Bath (scripture) and Zefa Picture Library (boy studying) for the cover photographs.

All other photographs supplied by the author.

Contents

This unit explains how the present Buddhist teaching began.

The Bodhisatta's life at the palace

The **Bodhisatta** (Bodhisattva) Prince Siddhattha Gotama (Siddhartha Gautama), the Buddha to be, was born in Lumbini in North India on the day of the full moon in May (Vesakha) in the 6th century BCE. Certain wise men said that if he were to see examples of unhappiness he would go in search of an answer and become a great religious leader. His father, King Suddhodhana, did not wish to lose an heir, so he arranged for the Prince to grow up in the palace cut off from any worries and from the troubles of ordinary people. At the age of sixteen the Prince was married to his beautiful cousin Princess Yasodhara. They lived a life of luxury, wanting for nothing in the way of palaces, clothes, food and entertainment. However, the Prince, reflecting on the quality of his life, was not entirely happy.

Then one day, while riding in his chariot in the city, he saw four sights he had not seen before. He saw an old man, a sick man and a dead body. On being questioned, his charioteer explained that this was the lot of all living beings. Prince Siddhattha was greatly disturbed. Then he saw a holy man, calm and serene. His charioteer explained that this was one who had given up worldly life and who was seeking an answer to the problem of suffering and the meaning of life.

Prince Siddhattha then decided that he too must set out to search for the meaning of life. He left the palace and its luxurious life, and at the age of 29 began to live the life of a holy man.

He went to several teachers and then spent some years with a group of five holy men. They lived a very hard life with little food, wearing only rags and living out in the open without any shelter, in order to pay more attention to spiritual development and less to bodily comfort. However, the Prince found that this type of life was not much help in finding an answer to his problem.

The Bodhisatta attains Enlightenment

In his early years the Prince had led a life of extreme luxury and after that a life of extreme hardship. But neither way of life seemed to have given him any satisfaction. He then decided on a middle way between a luxurious life and a hard life.

> 'There are these two extremes which should be avoided:
> 1 Indulgence in sensual pleasures and
> 2 Indulgence in extreme hardship.'
> (Dhammacakkappavattana Sutta)

On his own, and determined to succeed, Prince Siddhattha began to practise **meditation** (see Unit 21) under a **Bodhi tree**. He progressed in religious development, and at the age of 35 he attained

Four sacred places in India for Buddhist pilgrimage.

○ Lumbini – the birthplace of the Buddha

● Buddha Gaya – where the Buddha attained Enlightenment

◐ Isipatana – where the Buddha gave his first teaching

● Kusinara – where the Buddha passed away

began

Enlightenment by realizing the truth at Buddha Gaya, on the full-moon day in May.

He came to be known as Gotama Buddha. He taught for the rest of his life and started the order of the monks and nuns called the **Sangha** (see Units 6, 7 and 8). He passed away at Kusinara when he was 80 years old.

By his example and teaching the Gotama Buddha showed that the learning, understanding and practice of the teaching, contained today in the Buddhist scriptures, the word of the Buddha, was the most important thing for Buddhists.

He said:

> 'If you really want to see me, look at my Teaching.' (Samyutta Nikaya)

Speaking to Venerable Ananda at the end of his life, he said:

> 'When I am gone do not say that you have no teacher. Whatever I have taught let that be your teacher when I am gone.'
> (Mahaparinibbana Sutta)

Gotama Buddha attains Enlightenment under the Bodhi tree at Buddha Gaya in India.

His last words were:

> 'Everything is subject to change. Strive on with diligence.' (Mahaparinibbana Sutta)

Gotama Buddha's life story is told in the scriptures of different Buddhist traditions.

NEW WORDS

Bodhi tree the type of tree under which the Buddha attained Enlightenment

Bodhisatta (Bodhisattva)* a future Buddha, a person who has attained Enlightenment but postponed Nibbana (see Unit 2) to help others

Enlightenment realization of the truth of the way things are and the end of rebirth

Meditation mental control and development leading to concentration, calmness and wisdom

Sangha order of monks and nuns

* Some words have different spellings because of the different languages they come from, but they refer to the same thing. The two languages most important to the Buddhist scriptures are Pali and Sanskrit. For convenience we have chosen to use Pali spellings generally in this book.

On becoming a Buddha
'Through many a birth in existence wandered I
Seeking, but not finding, the builder of this house (body).
Sorrowful is repeated birth.
O craving you are seen. You shall build no house (body) again.
All your passions are broken. Your ignorance is shattered.
The mind attains Nibbana.
Achieved in the end of craving.'
(Dhammapada, v. 153.154)

2 The Buddha

This unit tells you about the Buddha.

The Buddha and the Dhamma

'Buddha' is the title given to a person who has experienced Enlightenment and who has seen the truth and the way things really are. The teachings of a Buddha come from his direct personal experience of reality, and are known as the **Dhamma** (Dharma). The Dhamma is the law which explains the true nature of everything that exists, both physical and non-physical, and is the true basis of reality.

In Buddhism there is no belief in a God who has created the world. The Dhamma is not a teaching given by such a God. Buddhism teaches that everyone is caught up in a cycle of birth, life, disease, old age, death and **Rebecoming** or Rebirth, caused by greed, hatred and ignorance. The aim of a Buddhist is to end this cycle by realizing the truth, that is by attaining Enlightenment and **Nibbana** (Nirvana). The Dhamma shows the way in which this can be done:

> 'You yourself must make the effort,
> The Buddhas are only teachers.'
> (Dhammapada, v. 276)

A large Buddha image, 50m high, at Buddhurajamaha Vihara, Dickwella, in Sri Lanka. In the foreground is 12-year-old Rahal.

After Enlightenment, a Buddha teaches the Dhamma, which continues in the world for a long time. Gradually over the years, the Dhamma is understood and practised less and less, and then it ceases to exist because it is forgotten. There is then a time when the Dhamma is not known in the world, until another Buddha attains Enlightenment and begins to teach. There is therefore a series of Buddhas and the Dhamma they all teach is the same.

Some traditions of Buddhism consider the Buddha to be a human being, but an extraordinary person, who has attained mental and spiritual powers far beyond those of ordinary human beings. Other traditions also regard the Buddha as a human being, and have developed the idea of a permanent and continuing spiritual Buddha who can appear in the world as a Buddha or in another form.

Many Buddhas

Each Buddha goes through many human and non-human lives in preparation for becoming a Buddha. In these lives he is known as a Bodhisatta. The present teaching is that of Gotama Buddha or Sakyamuni Buddha. There were Buddhas before him and there will be Buddhas to come. Gotama Buddha explained that the Buddha who came before him was Kassapa Buddha and the next Buddha to come is Maitreya Buddha, who now lives in a heavenly world until he is born in the human world to attain Enlightenment.

An 8th-century Buddha image in a cave temple at Sokkuran, South Korea.

Since the Dhamma is not of divine origin but is the content and meaning of the scriptures, which are the word of the Buddha, the practice of the teaching has special importance. The Buddha said:

> 'He honours me best who practises my teaching best.'   (Maha Parinibbana Sutta)

He urged Buddhists to pay more attention to the teaching and less attention to himself as a person.

The Buddha asked his followers not to accept the Dhamma simply because it was taught by a Buddha, but to practise it and test it to see whether it is true.

> 'You have been instructed by me about this timeless doctrine which can be realized and verified and understood individually by the intelligent.'   (Majjhima Nikaya)

The Dhamma can be summarized like this:

> 'To avoid all evil, to do good, to purify one's mind – that is the teaching of the Buddhas.'
> (Dhammapada, v.183)

NEW WORDS

Dhamma (Dharma) the teaching of a Buddha

Nibbana (Nirvana) realization of the truth of the way things are and the end of rebirth

Rebecoming Rebirth, or the continuity of life after death

Nibbana
'Enslaved by greed, enraged by anger, blinded by delusion, overwhelmed, with a mind ensnared, man aims at his own ruin, at the ruin of others, at the ruin of both, and he experiences mental pain and grief. But if greed, anger and delusion are given up, man aims neither at his own ruin, nor at the ruin of others, nor at the ruin of both, and he experiences no mental pain or grief. This is Nibbana immediate, visible in this life, inviting, attractive and able to be understood by the wise.'   (Anguttara Nikaya)

3 Chanting the Dhamma

This unit tells you about the memorized oral tradition and the importance of chanting to Buddhists.

Oral teaching

In his lifetime the Buddha's teaching was oral (spoken). The place where he lived was called Magadha and the language he spoke was called Magadhi. This was a spoken form of Sanskrit, one of the classical languages in India. The Buddha advised the Sangha to teach in the language of the people they spoke to. As Buddhism spread to various parts of India, Asia and the world, the Dhamma was translated into various other languages.

Memory training was, and still is, an important part of education in India. The Sangha memorized the teaching, some of them possibly specialising in certain parts of it. There were group recitations of the teaching at festivals and other special occasions. These group or communal recitations helped the Sangha to remember the teaching. If one of them had forgotten a part he could learn it during the recitation. This oral tradition depended on a continuous stream of teachers passing down the teaching to students. The teaching was handed down from generation to generation accurately by means of these group recitations.

Agreement of the teaching

Three months after the Buddha's passing away a conference of senior members of the Sangha, called the First Council, was held at Rajagaha, the capital of Magadha. One monk, Ven. Upali, explained and recited the Vinaya (monastic rules) and another, Ven. Ananda, recited the Dhamma (the teaching). The 500 members of the Council then agreed on the wording. This division of the teaching into Vinaya and Dhamma had come into existence during the lifetime of the Buddha.

About 100 years later a Second Council was held at Vesali. Again the Vinaya and the Dhamma were recited and agreed upon. Although differences arose later, the Sangha were united at this time. The Vinaya and the Dhamma agreed at the Second Council form the foundation of the teaching in all the traditions of Buddhism.

The oral tradition of Buddhism continues today. The Sangha memorize sections of the Dhamma and chant portions of it at festivals and ceremonies, both in the temples and in the homes of Buddhists. Though the occasion differs, what is recited is more or less the same. This chanting is considered to be a sacred act. It also helps to teach children and adults because after hearing it several times, they begin to remember the words. They also associate the different circumstances and

A special structure called a mandappa, built inside a house in Sri Lanka to accommodate monks chanting Pirit.

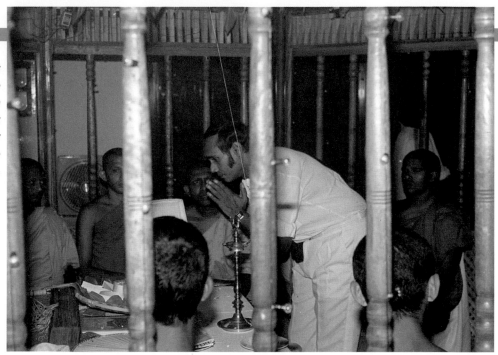

Kirtilal, a Buddhist devotee, invites the monks to begin chanting at a Pirit (blessing) ceremony in his new home in Sri Lanka.

occasions of chanting. Sometimes the **lay people** join in the chanting. Many Buddhists find the chanting a meditative and **devotional** experience. The sound of chanting has a calming effect on the mind. Modern day Buddhists listen to cassettes of chanting at home and in their cars.

Many Buddhists feel that reciting and listening to the chanting of specially selected texts from the scriptures, or **Pirit**, is a blessing, gives them protection, and produces a sense of mental well-being. In Sri Lanka on special occasions, such as moving into a new house, a Pirit ceremony is arranged, sometimes overnight, as a blessing. In Japan, Nichiren Buddhists chant the title of the Lotus Sutra in Japanese, 'Namu Myoho Renge Kyo' (I seek refuge in the Lotus Sutra) at their worship and also long passages of the Sutra. The spelling 'Sutra' is used in the title of a Sanskrit text, and '**Sutta**' is used in the title of a Pali text. In Tibet the chanting of 'Om Mani Padme Hum' (Hail the Jewel in the Lotus) is often accompanied by ritual gestures to increase the effect of the spoken words.

In all Buddhist communities chanting is part of the funeral service to bless the dead person. This is especially important as Buddhists believe in the continuity of life. In Japan the Pure Land Buddhists have a ritual chant called the Nembutsu, 'Namu Amida Butsu' (Praise the Amida Buddha).

NEW WORDS

Devotional in the nature of worship

Lay people people who are not ordained

Pirit selected scriptures, or chanting them, which gives protection

Sutta (Sutra) a Dhamma text (see Units 4 and 5)

Happiness

'He who, whilst seeking happiness,
Does not trouble and punish others
Who are also seeking happiness
Will find happiness in the other world.'

'Perform faithfully the precepts of the Dhamma
Abstain from all evil deeds
He who keeps the Dhamma finds happiness
In this world and in the other.'

'He who keeps the Dhamma in guarded by the Dhamma.'

(The Udanavarga – Tibetan scriptures)

This unit tells you about the geographical expansion of Buddhism.

The Tipitaka

Some time after the Second Council (see Unit 3) there was a division in the Sangha between the Elders, or Sthaviras, and other monks known as the Great Community or Mahasanghas. In the years that followed new **sects** arose from these main divisions.

A Third Council was held during the time of the Emperor Asoka of India (269–32BCE). The teaching was, again, recited and agreed. The first two parts were the same as before: the Vinaya Pitaka (monastic rules) and the Sutta Pitaka (the Dhamma). Sutta (Sutra) originally meant string or thread. In Buddhist teaching it came to mean a text which was short and could be understood without further explanations. Now a third section, the Abhidhamma Pitaka was added. The Abhidhamma or the 'further' Dhamma contained analysis and explanations of the teaching. The different schools and traditions of Buddhism generally share the main parts of the Vinaya and the Sutta Pitakas, but each developed the Abhidhamma Pitaka in its own way.

The sections were referred to as Pitaka. Pitaka means 'basket' – a container for, or a collection of, texts. The three sections are known as the Tipitaka.

Buddhist Asia.

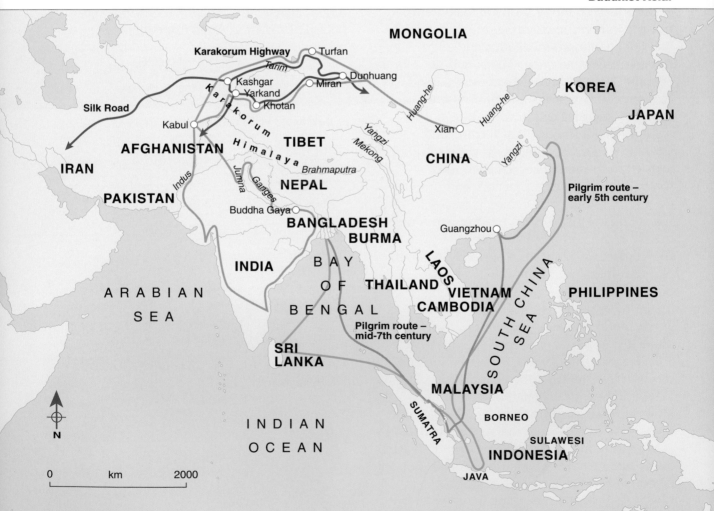

world

Buddhism spreads beyond India

Buddhism continued to flourish in India until about the 11th century CE. At the end of the Third Council missions were sent to different parts of India, Sri Lanka and to other countries nearby to teach Buddhism. The tradition of Buddhism which went to Sri Lanka from India was called **Theravada** (Teaching of the Elders). From India and Sri Lanka the Theravada teaching reached other South Asian countries such as Burma, Malaysia, Thailand, Cambodia, Laos, Vietnam and Indonesia. Buddhism reached Central Asia and China from India, went from China to Korea, and from Korea to Japan. Buddhism went to Tibet from India and China, and from there to Mongolia. The teaching was written down in most of these countries in the local languages (see Unit 5).

Mahayana Buddhism began in India about 100BCE and developed certain new ideas. New Suttas were written, mainly between 100BCE and 400BCE, in the same form as the earlier Suttas setting out Mahayana ideas, and were given special importance. Most Mahayana Buddhists consider the Lotus Sutra to be the highest point of their teaching.

'Just as the great ocean surpasses all springs, streams and tanks, so the Lotus of the True Law surpasses all Sutras spoken by the Buddhas.' (The Lotus Sutra)

Tantric Buddhism developed within Mahayana Buddhism in India in about the 5th century CE. All forms of Buddhism went to Tibet. Tantric Buddhism had the most influence there. The Buddhism of Tibet is called **Vajrayana** Buddhism.

From early times Buddhism has been a major religion in Russia, especially in the Central Asian and Eastern parts. Over the last century Buddhism went from Japan to the Americas, especially to the west coasts. There was an interest in Buddhism among the people in Europe from about 1820CE and translations were made of some scriptures. In this century Buddhism has become established as a religion in the West.

NEW WORDS

Mahayana 'great or wide vehicle or career'; a school of Buddhism which now includes the different Buddhist traditions dominant in the Far East

Sects traditions within a religion

Theravada 'teaching of the Elders'; a school of Buddhism based on the Pali Canon (see Unit 5) now in south Asian countries

Vajrayana 'thunderbolt or diamond vehicle or career'; the tradition of Buddhism in Tibet

One Buddha Vehicle
'Knowing the supreme Nibbana
Though by reason of their tactful powers
They teach various kinds of ways,
Really they are but the One Buddha Vehicle.
Knowing the conduct of all creatures,
What they think in their deepest minds,
The Karma they have developed in the past
Their inclinations and interest,
And their capacities, keen or dull,
with various kinds of reasonings…
Now I also in like manner…
Proclaim the Buddha way.' (Lotus Sutra)

5 The scriptures are written down

This unit tells you how some Buddhist scriptures came to be written down.

Pali and Sanskrit scriptures

The teaching of Theravada Buddhism in Sri Lanka was in Pali, a language from Western India. Pali is a spoken language with no script of its own, so it can be written in any script.

In about 30BCE a Council was held in Sri Lanka and in order to preserve the teaching it was written down in Pali. The writing was in three sections: the Vinaya Pitaka, the Sutta Pitaka and the Abhidhamma Pitaka (see Unit 4), known together as the Tipitaka (three baskets). This was the first time Buddhist teaching had been written down. It is called the Pali scriptures or **canon**.

The writing was on strips of dried palm leaves cut into rectangles and etched with a metal stylus and rubbed over with carbon ink. Writing and copying the teaching by hand is considered a **worthy activity** and even today the Sangha carry on this practice.

In India Buddhist teaching was first written down in the 1st century CE. It was written in Sanskrit and is known as the Sanskrit scriptures or canon, the Tripitaka.

The Chinese scriptures

The translation of the Suttas into Chinese began in about 200CE and went on for over 1000 years. At first the translators were non-Chinese monks working with Chinese assistants. Later they were Chinese monks. Some Suttas were translated and re-translated several times. It was difficult translating Sanskrit into Chinese and expressing some of the ideas to fit in with Chinese culture. Original Chinese Suttas were also added.

These scriptures were written in carbon ink on paper. Sometimes gold and silver ink was used on dark blue paper. Suttas were also engraved on polished stone and rock, on cavern walls and on slate tablets, and some can still be seen today.

I take Refuge in the Buddha
English

බුද්ධං සරණං ගච්ඡාමි
Pali (Sinhala script)

Buddham Saranam Gacchami
Pali (Roman script)

बुद्धम् सरणम् गच्छामि
Sanskrit

Tibetan (script)

Sangye la kapsu cheo
Tibetan (pronunciation)

Ishin chōrai, Jippō hōkai, Jyōjū Butsu
Japanese (pronunciation)

一心頂禮十方法界常住佛
Japanese (script)

Some languages and scripts of the Buddhist scriptures.

Pictures and words from the copy of the Diamond Sutra, the oldest printed book in existence, which is kept in the British Museum.

Copying the Sutras by hand was a long and tiring job and so the Chinese began to think of ways to make copies of the Sutras more conveniently. In about the 8th century CE they thought out that if 'mirror-images' of Chinese characters were carved on blocks of wood these could be used to print several copies of a Sutra. This was the invention of wood block printing. The oldest printed book in existence is the Diamond Sutra, dated 868CE, a copy of which is in the British Library in London.

Other scriptures

Buddhism also has scriptures in other languages, including Japanese, Korean, Tibetan and Mongolian. The whole of the Pali scriptures have been translated into English.

The Chinese scriptures are now being translated into English. Some of the scriptures have also been translated into other European languages.

NEW WORDS

Canon a collection of sacred books accepted as genuine

Worthy activity work which, according to Buddhist teaching, has good consequences

Last instructions

'O monks do not feel despondent. If I were to live in this world for a very long time, my association with you would still come to an end, since a meeting with no parting is an impossibility. The Dhamma is now complete for each and every one....

'From now on, all my disciples must continue to practise without ceasing. But as to the world, nothing there is eternal, so that all meetings must be followed by partings. So, do not harbour grief, for such is the nature of worldly things. But do strive diligently and speedily seek for freedom. With the light of Perfect Wisdom destroy the darkness of ignorance, for in this world nothing is strong or enduring.' (Buddha Pachchimovada Parinibbana Sutra – Chinese scripture)

6 Vinaya and the Sangha I

In this unit and the next Ven. Dhammaseela, a member of the Sangha, answers questions asked by 12-year-old Phi Khong, a Buddhist from Beijing in China. All the answers are taken from the Vinaya Pitaka, a part of the Buddhist scriptures, and Buddhist practice today.

The Sangha and their rules (Vinaya)

Q: Who are the Sangha?

A: The word 'Sangha' at first included monks, nuns, lay men and lay women. But today it refers only to the Order of monks and nuns founded by Gotama Buddha. The Sangha still exist in a direct unbroken line from the Buddha. They form the third element of the **Triple Gem** (see Unit 19). It is the Sangha who preserve and continue the teaching.

Q: What are the monastic rules?

A: The Buddha defined the monastic rules (regarding the organization, conduct and discipline) in order to guide and regulate the Sangha. These rules are known as the Vinaya (see Unit 3). The first part of the Vinaya Pitaka consists of the rules of conduct, known collectively as Patimokkha, and explanations

of these rules. The second part gives the rules regarding admission to the order, fortnightly meetings and recital of Patimokkha, seclusion during the rainy season (**Vassa**), medicine, food, ceremonies, robes, the manner of dealing with offences, dwellings, lodgings, how to do deal with differences of opinion, travel, duties of teachers and novices, the **ordination** of nuns and the history of the first two Councils: a complete and comprehensive guide for the Sangha.

Ordination

Q: What is ordination?

A: Admission to the order is by an ordination ceremony. Anyone worthy of admission and in good health can be ordained. First there is a novice ordination when new members undertake the rules, then the training and finally the higher ordination. On ordination a person cuts off all social relations with family and friends. This is generally for life, but a member may leave the order whenever he or she wishes. In Burma, Thailand, Laos and Cambodia there is a widespread custom of short-term ordination. Lay men may become ordained as novices for a week or a few months, live as members of

An ordination ceremony in Sri Lanka.

the Sangha and learn the Dhamma. This may be done several times during a lifetime. The Sangha is a self-regulating body governed by two rules:

1 those senior by ordination take precedence, and
2 all important decisions are taken by agreement or by majority decision.

Q: Who is the head of the Sangha?

A: There is no central authority, but generally the monks and nuns in a temple or monastery belong to a larger group which will have a senior monk or nun who might exercise some authority. In Thailand and some countries of South East Asia the Sangha are organized as a national institution and a Sangharaja is appointed as the head of the Sangha.

Ven. Myokyo-ni, a senior nun in the Zen tradition, writes:

'Vinaya – the **Precepts** – differ in number for monks and lay people. They are not "commandments" but are undertaken voluntarily. At their most basic, they remind us not to do harm to others or ourselves, whether intentionally as in a temper, or from lack of consideration for others, whether to fellow human beings, animals or a cup or broom. This means cultivating a caring attitude rather than "doing my thing" regardless. Kindness and good will to all things have their root in this attitude which can then be further cultivated.

There is no game of play without rules, whether football or a board game or games children play. As children we were eager to learn the rules so as to be able to play together. And if one did not abide by the rules, wanting exceptions, one was a spoil-sport, spoiling the game and pleasure for all, oneself included!

So as not to become selfish and self-centred spoil-sports and consequently suffer from lack

Teaching calligraphy at a monastery in China.

of relationship and communication, we turn to the Precepts as supports to help us play the game of being decent human beings, respectful and considerate of each other and thus contributing to our mutual happiness and peace.' (For Precepts see Unit 14.)

NEW WORDS

Ordination ceremony for entering the order
Precepts rules of conduct or guidelines
Triple Gem the Buddha, Dhamma and Sangha
Vassa seclusion during the rainy season

Advice to the Sangha

'So long as the monks and nuns shall be full of faith, modest in heart, afraid of wrongdoing, full of learning, strong in energy, active in mind, and full of wisdom…

'So long as the monks and nuns shall exercise themselves in the sevenfold higher wisdom, that is to say, in mental activity, search after truth, energy, joy, peace, earnest contemplation, and evenness of mind – so long may you be expected not to decline, but to prosper.'   (Maha Parinibbana Sutta)

7 Vinaya and the Sangha II

In this unit Ven. Dhammaseela, a member of the Sangha, answers more questions asked by 12-year-old Phi Khong, a Buddhist from Beijing in China.

The work of the Sangha

Q: What do monks and nuns actually do ?
A: The Buddha said:

> 'Go forth, O Monks, for the good of the many, for the welfare of the many; out of compassion for the world teach this Dhamma which is glorious in the beginning, glorious in the middle and glorious at the end, in the spirit and in the letter.'
>
> (Vinaya Pitaka, Mahavagga)

That is what we do; we teach the Dhamma. The monks and nuns set an example of a good Buddhist life and we are living evidence of the teaching. Over the years in various countries, in Asia and outside, differences have arisen in the status and activities of the monks and nuns. These are due to social, economic, geographical and political reasons.

Differences in the traditions

Q: What sorts of differences do you refer to?
A: In the Theravada tradition the monks and nuns continue the custom of meeting on Uposatha days, full-moon and new-moon days. When they meet they recite the Vinaya rules and confess any breach of the rules. This was given up in the Mahayana countries more than 1000 years ago. Again, in the Theravada tradition the monks and nuns are strict about having their main meal before noon, while in other, colder countries they have a light evening meal.

In the Theravada countries and in China the monks and nuns do not marry. In Japan generally the ordained persons, referred to as priests, monks or ministers, marry and have families, except in a few traditions such as Zen.

In Tibet there are several types of the Sangha. Monks and nuns live in monasteries and do not marry. But some part-time monks have families and spend only a part of the year in a monastery. The Lamas (religious teachers) are recognized as Bodhisattas (see Unit 11) who have a relationship between their present lives and previous lives. Tibet is unusual in having the offices of the religious and political Heads of State vested in the office of His Holiness, The Dalai Lama. The present holder of the office is Ven. Tenzin Gyatso, The Fourteenth Dalai Lama. A Dalai Lama is considered to be the Reincarnation of the previous holder of the office, and also the

Buddhist nuns studying the scriptures at Amaravati Buddhist Centre in England.

A Soto Zen novice monk from Eiheiji, Japan, dressed to go on a pilgrimage.

Rev. Daishin Morgan, of the Order of Buddhist Contemplatives in Throssel Hole Priory, England, writes:

'For me as a monk the Vinaya shows how the spirit of the Buddha's teaching has been put into practice within monastic life. The stories of why the various rules were made are encouraging because they show that monks in the Buddha's day made just as many mistakes as we do today, and if they still managed to reach Enlightenment then so can I! I believe it is the underlying principles expressed in the rules that are most important, rather than being concerned with following the letter of the rules exactly. However, any changes must be done with the greatest care otherwise the spirit gets lost.'

Bhikkhu Seevali, a Nepalese monk trained in the Theravada tradition, writes:

'To help one to be restrained in what one says, to control the body and to develop one's mind is the role of the Vinaya. It uplifts a person's life from normal to the enlightened way. If the culture of the mind and the body is no longer practised, the Buddhist community will come to an end. For monks, nuns and lay folk the Buddha laid down the disciplinary rules to mould and shape their lives along the path to Enlightenment.'

Monks and nuns

'The monk who lives in the Dhamma, who delights in the Dhamma, who meditates on the Dhamma, who well remembers the Dhamma, does not fall away from the splendid Dhamma.

'He who has no thought of "I and mine" whatever towards mind and body, he who grieves not for that which he has not, he is indeed called a monk.'

(The Dhammapada, v. 364, 367)

Reincarnation of the Bodhisattva Avalokitesvara.

Nepal, again, has different types of the Sangha. There are scholar teacher priests (vajracaryas) and monks. It is quite usual for them to follow professions outside the monastery, to have families and live in houses near the temples.

This unit tells you how the scriptures determine the lives of Theravada monks and nuns.

A disciplined and simple life

Monks (**bhikkhus**) and nuns (**bhikkhunis**) – the Sangha – are directly linked with the Buddha. They lead a life of self-control, study and meditation. They practise and teach the Dhamma, and attend to the religious needs of the lay people. They live in a **vihara** (monastery or nunnery).

The Buddha's stepmother, Prajapati Gotami, requested him to ordain women. But because of the social conditions in India at that time, where women had a less important place in society, the Buddha was at first reluctant to do so. Then Ven. Ananda took up the cause:

'"Are women, Sir, capable of realising the highest fruits of the teaching (Nibbana)?

"They are so capable, Ananda."

"If then, Sir, they are so capable, since Prajapati Gotami looked after you so well when you were small after your mother's passing away, why not ordain her?"

"If she accepts the extra rules let her be ordained", said the Buddha, and formulated extra rules to protect the order of nuns.'
(Vinaya Pitaka, Cullavagga)

The Vinaya rules say that the monks and nuns must dress modestly, in robes, and not try to make themselves look attractive or adorn themselves:

'You are not to wear ear rings, bangles, necklaces and rings. You are not to have long hair.' (Vinaya Pitaka, Cullavagga)

Daily life

The monks and nuns get up before sunrise. First they clean the vihara where they live. Then they pay homage to the Buddha and do formal meditation for a set period of time (see Unit 21). After breakfast, given as alms by lay people or prepared by themselves, they spend time memorizing the Suttas.

Lay **devotees** come to the vihara during the day and in the evening to learn and discuss the Dhamma, to ask for advice, to take the Three Refuges and to listen to Pirit chanting (see Units 3 and 19). After Pirit a monk will tie an orange coloured Pirit thread round the wrist of the devotee as a blessing and protection. The three strands of the thread stand for the Three Refuges: The Buddha, Dhamma and Sangha (see Unit 19).

The monks and nuns then take their bowls and go on an alms round. This is not begging. It gives lay people an opportunity to show their respect and devotion by giving food (**dana**) to

A devotee giving alms (food) to a monk in Sri Lanka.

nuns (Sangha)

the Sangha. Sometimes lay people invite a group of the Sangha to their homes, or bring the dana to the vihara. This happens when a dana is being given for a special reason, such as in memory of a relative who has passed away.

The midday meal is taken before noon, to fit in with the monastic life. No solid food is taken after midday; only drinks like tea or soup. The Vinaya gives instructions as to how monks and nuns should eat. Some of these are:

> 'Eat the alms placed in the bowl.'
> 'Do not ask for more food.'
> 'Do not envy what others are eating.'
> 'Do not talk with food in the mouth.'
> 'Eat without smacking the lips.'
> (Vinaya Pitaka, Patimokka)

After the meal the monks and nuns may rest a while. They do not play organized games like tennis. Instead, to exercise, they walk and clean the garden. This is done as a form of meditation. They may not:

> '...dig the ground or have it dug...'
> '...destroy any plant or tree...'
> '...pollute the garden, stream, pond or any other place.'   (Vinaya Pitaka, Patimokka)

The afternoon may be spent in meeting visitors to the vihara, reading and studying. Sometimes they visit schools and colleges to give talks on Buddhism. They visit people who are ill, either at home or in hospital, and they also visit people in prisons. Often in the

Evening worship at a temple on Jiuha Shan, the 'Nine Flower Mountain' in China.

early evening monks and nuns teach in the Dhamma classes or conduct meditation sessions in the vihara.

Each night the monks and nuns in the vihara come together and chant the Suttas. Generally this is done at a set time and lay people may also attend.

The last part of the day is devoted to private study and meditation, and they usually go to bed at about 10.00 p.m.

NEW WORDS

Bhikkhu Buddhist monk

Bhikkhuni Buddhist nun

Dana giving of money, time, goods etc. to the Sangha, generally alms or food

Devotee person who follows a religious way of life

Vihara Buddhist temple, monastery or nunnery

Monk or nun

'Not cultivating any thought of sense satisfaction,
His senses subdued and perfectly freed,
Without selfishness or attachment to a home,
Having cast off desires and living in solitude,
Such a man is a monk.

'Associating only with the pure in living,
With those who are without laziness,
Observing the different precepts of the Dhamma,
One will learn the essential rules of life.

'He who controls his hands and feet,
Who controls his speech and his senses,
Who finds all his pleasure in solitude,
Who is contented, him I call a monk.'
(The Udanavarga – Tibetan scriptures)

9 The Four Noble Truths

This unit tells you about the use of the scriptures for teaching the **Four Noble Truths**.

Gotama Buddha understood that the truths which he had realized on Enlightenment were common to all beings. He saw that there were some who could understand the truth and decided to teach what he had realized. The Buddha's first teaching was to his friends, the five holy men (see Unit 1), and the assembled deities in the Deer Park at Isipatana in Benares. It was on the full-moon day in July, eight weeks after he attained Enlightenment. This teaching is called the Teaching on Turning the Wheel of Truth. In this teaching the Buddha dealt with the problem of unsatisfactoriness or suffering and explained the Four Noble Truths:

1   Life is Dukkha.
Dukkha has a range of meanings including suffering, imperfection, impermanence, discomfort, boredom and so on. If one word is needed 'unsatisfactoriness' seems to be the best.

> 'Birth is suffering, ageing is suffering, sickness is suffering, death is suffering, association with the unpleasant is suffering, separation from the pleasant is suffering, not to get what one desires is suffering.'

2   Dukkha is caused by selfishness, greed or craving.

> 'It is this greed which produces rebecoming (rebirth), clinging to this and that (life) and craving for sensual pleasures, craving for existing and craving for non-existence.'

The Noble Eightfold Path – a diagram.

1 Right *Understanding or Views*	**I** *Morality,* or Love or True respect for oneself and others
2 Right *Thoughts or Intentions*	
3 Right *Speech*	
4 Right *Actions*	**II** *Mental Development,* or Mental discipline or Meditation
5 Right *Livelihood*	
6 Right *Effort*	
7 Right *Mindfulness*	**III** *Wisdom*
8 Right *Concentration*	

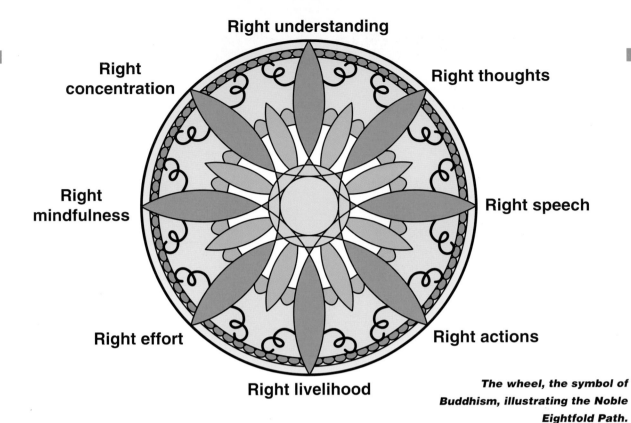

Right understanding

Right thoughts

Right concentration

Right speech

Right mindfulness

Right actions

Right effort

Right livelihood

The wheel, the symbol of Buddhism, illustrating the Noble Eightfold Path.

3 If this greed is overcome or transcended (risen above) then Dukkha is ended. The Buddha spoke of

'the complete separation from, and destruction of, this very craving, giving it up, liberating oneself from it.'

This is Nibbana, the end of Rebirth and Rebecoming, and the end of the sense of self.

4 The way to achieve this is to follow the **Noble Eightfold Path**.

'It is the Noble Eightfold Path, namely right understanding, right thoughts, right speech, right actions, right livelihood, right effort, right mindfulness, right concentration.'

The diagram explains the Noble Eightfold path. The three stages to reach this goal are morality, mental development and wisdom, but they must be practised at the same time. The wheel is a symbol of Buddhism. It is shown with eight spokes to represent the Noble Eightfold Path.

NEW WORDS

Dukkha nature of being unsatisfactory, suffering

Four Noble Truths four of the most important elements of the Buddhist teaching

Noble Eightfold Path the path to be followed by a Buddhist, the Middle Way

Mindfulness

'How do men and gods avoid religious downfall? They observe mindfulness. What is mindfulness? Mindfulness consists in guarding the mind; giving up wrong things; abandoning worldly pleasures and depending on the pleasure of the Dharma; not giving way to harmful mental desires, not giving way to nonvirtuous mental activities, such as greed, hatred, or ignorance; not performing injurious actions with body, speech, and mind in short, avoiding religious downfall.' (Guhya-acittavyapti Sutra – Tibetan scripture)

10 The Three Signs of Being

This unit tells you about the use of the scriptures for teaching the Three Signs of Being.

There was more to be explained to the five holy men (see Unit 9). So the Buddha decided to give them further teaching. In this teaching, called the Teaching of No-Self, he explained what Buddhists call the Three Signs of Being or Three Characteristics of Existence.

1 Impermanence (Anicca)

The Buddha realized and taught that nothing in the world is permanent. Everything, all mental and physical states, are changing all the time.

You are not the same person as you were before reading Unit 9 because you now know about the Four Noble Truths, which you did not know before. Very soon you will know about the Three Signs of Being and then you will be a different person to what you are now. Therefore your mind is constantly changing. The chair on which you sit will not be there in a few years' time, as it will break up. All physical things are also changing. In most cases the rate of change is so slow that you cannot notice the changes.

> '"What do you think, monks, is this body permanent or impermanent?"
>
> "Impermanent, Sir."
>
> "Is that which is impermanent happy or painful?"
>
> "It is painful (dukkha), Sir."'

Impermanence is also explained elsewhere in the scriptures:

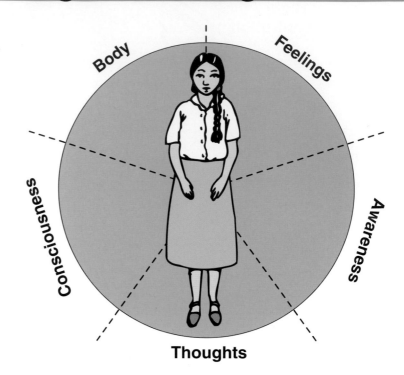

The five elements of a person.

> 'Anything that is born, brought into being and organized, contains within itself the character that it will change and dissolve.'
>
> (Maha Parinibbana Sutta)

2 Dukkha (explained in Unit 9)
3 Selflessness (Anatta)

A living being has no self or soul, meaning a permanent, unchanging, spiritual entity created by God or having a divine source. A living being is a grouping of constantly changing physical and mental forces which can be explained in this way:

> 'The body is not self; feelings are not self; in like manner awareness, thoughts, and consciousness are not self. These must be understood in their true nature as being not mine...not I...not my self.'

These forces are kept active by greed and selfishness. They come to an end when this is overcome by attaining Nibbana, through practising the Noble Eightfold Path. To Buddhists this is a law of nature. The Buddhas

'The first teaching', a Burmese painting.

do not think it out. They realize it and then teach it.

> 'Whether Buddhas appear or not, O monks, it remains a fact that all **conditioned** (compound) things are impermanent (anicca), dukkha and that everything is selfless (anatta).'　(Anguttara Nikaya)

NEW WORDS

Anatta without soul, self or ego

Anicca impermanent, changing

Conditioned made up of other things

Impermanence

'Alas! the life energies are impermanent,
What is created must indeed perish,
What is born must meet death,
In calmness alone is there happiness....

'As a river running swiftly
Can never turn back on itself
So too with the days of a person's life,
They vanish and come back no more....

'So take constant joy in calm meditation,
Strive earnestly, seeing the end of birth and age.'　(The Udanavarga – Tibetan scriptures)

This unit tells you about the use of the scriptures for teaching some of the ideas of the Mahayana and Vajrayana schools of Buddhism.

Bodhisatta Tara, a 12th-century image found in Sri Lanka.

The Lotus Sutra

Most Mahayana Buddhists (see Unit 4) consider the Lotus Sutra to be the highest point of their teaching. The first part deals with the nature of people and existence, and the second deals with the nature of the Buddhas.

This Sutra teaches certain important Mahayana ideas:

1 All beings can achieve Buddhahood by following the teaching in the Sutra.

2 All living things, including human beings, are of the great life force of the Universe and are equal.

3 The Buddha is eternal and appears in many forms from time to time.

4 The Bodhisatta path, where one devotes oneself to helping others to attain Nibbana, is the highest.

5 There is only one path within Buddhism – **Buddhayana**, the Path of a Buddha.

6 The equal status of lay and ordained persons.

'After entering (Nirvana by knowing this Sutra), putting on his robe and sitting down on the seat, the Bodhisattva should teach this Sutra. The strength of kindness is my home, compassion is my robe, void is my seat.'

The Lotus Sutra sets out the duties of a teacher of the Dhamma – receiving and keeping the Sutras, reading, reciting, teaching and copying them.

Emptiness and wisdom

Mahayana Buddhism develops the ideas of emptiness (**Sunyata**) and wisdom (**Prajna**). Emptiness means that persons and things have no permanent, fixed and independent nature. They have no substance and therefore they are empty or non-substantial. For instance, think of a bicycle. It is called a bicycle because the wheels, frame, handlebars and seat are fitted together to form what we call a bicycle. If they are taken apart there is no bicycle. Therefore the idea of a bicycle is really empty.

Vajrayana Buddhism

'Avalokatisvera as Guide of Souls', a 10th-century banner painting from China.

'Form is emptiness and emptiness is form. The same is true of feelings, awareness, thoughts and consciousness.'
(Heart Sutra and Diamond Sutra)

Wisdom or Buddha wisdom is the higher level of understanding and experience. Wisdom is the last of the six practices which Mahayana Buddhists undertake in order to achieve Enlightenment.

The Bodhisatta

Another idea which has developed is that the Bodhisatta is someone who has postponed Nibbana in order to help others on the Buddhist path.

'As many beings as there are in the Universe of beings, all these I must lead to Nirvana.'
(Diamond Sutra)

'Whatever brings benefit and joy to all living beings, that I (the Bodhisattva) will accomplish.' (Arya-dharma-samgiti Sutra)
(Tibetan Scriptures)

Tibetan teaching

In addition to the teachings of the other schools, Tibetan Buddhism (Vajrayana) (*see* Unit 4) features special oral teaching handed down from teacher to pupil, initiation ceremonies, elaborate rituals and complex meditations developed in stages. There is a very special and unique relationship between the teacher and the pupil because of this method of teaching.

'Do not despise your teacher
Do not stray from the Buddha's teaching
Do not criticise or feel anger toward your fellows
Do not give up the Bodhi-mind.'
(Krsnayamari Tantra)

NEW WORDS

Buddhayana Buddha path or career, a combination of the teachings of all the Buddhist traditions

Prajna wisdom in relation to the Buddhist teaching

Sunyata emptiness, not substantial

Emptiness

'Therefore, O Sariputra, in emptiness there is no form, nor feeling, nor perception, nor impulse, nor consciousness; no eye, ear, nose, tongue, body, mind; no forms, sounds, smells, tastes, touchables or objects of mind...no ignorance, no ending of ignorance...there is no decay and death, no ending of decay and death; there is no suffering, no beginning, no stopping, no path; no understanding, no attainment, and no non-attainment.' (Heart Sutra)

12 The story of Kisa Gotami

This unit tells you how the Buddha taught by giving a person a task to perform.

Your teacher sometimes explains lessons to you and sometimes gives you some work or a project to do. The Buddha also taught in this way, sometimes by asking a person to do some work. The story of Kisa Gotami is a good example of this. It is taken from the Buddhist scriptures and illustrates fundamental Buddhist ideas like Dukkha, impermanence and that death comes to everyone (see Units 9 and 10).

'Kisa Gotami's son

During the Buddha's time there lived a lady called Kisa Gotami. A son was born to her. She looked after him with great love and care. However, the child died as soon as he was able to walk. His mother was grief-stricken.

Kisa Gotami carries her dead son from house to house.

'It is a Buddhist practice to cremate a dead body. The mother, who had not seen death before, did not allow the body of her beloved son to be cremated. She thought that her son was ill and wanted to find some medicine to bring him back to life.

'The mother went from house to house carrying the body of her dead son asking, "Have you got some medicine to cure my son?" The people replied, "That boy is dead, no medicine will bring him back to life." Finally she came to the house of a wise man. He felt that he should help her and said, "I do not know of any such medicine, but go and ask Gotama Buddha, he will tell you of a suitable medicine."

'So she went to the Buddha and asked him if he knew of a medicine to cure her son. "Yes" said the Buddha, "I know of a medicine for this purpose. Go and get some mustard seeds from a house in which no one has died."

'Kisa Gotami thanked the Buddha and, carrying the body of her dead son, went in search of mustard seeds. At each house, she said, "The Buddha has asked me to bring some mustard seeds from a house in which no one has died, as medicine for my dead son. Is this such a house?" The householders replied, "We are very sorry but one of our family died in this house some time ago." This was the reply she had at every house in the town. Therefore she could not get any mustard seeds.

'The lesson Kisa Gotami learned
She realized that in every house and in every family someone had died. She realized that in the whole town the number of people who had died was more than those who were living.

'Kisa Gotami went to the Buddha and said, "It is impossible, Sir, to get the mustard seeds which you asked me to get. Someone has died in every house and in every family." The Buddha explained that his medicine was really for her, and not for her son, "You imagined that only your son was dead, but it is the constant lot of beings." He explained the Dhamma to her and spoke this verse:

"Death seizes and carries away
The worldly man, whose mind
Is set on families and on owning herds (of cattle),
As a great flood (carries away) a sleeping village."   (The Dhammapada, v. 287)

'The Buddha granted her request to be admitted into the order of nuns. Later, on a day when it was her turn to light the lamp in the meeting hall, she observed the flame. She noticed the movement and continuity of the flame and remarked:

"Even so it is with living creatures, they rise and pass away, and on attaining Nibbana they are no more known."

'The Buddha understood her thoughts and said:

"Rather than live a hundred years,
But not achieve Nibbana,
Better is the life of a single day
For him who sees Nibbana."
                    (The Dhammapada, v. 114)'

This story is found in the book of stories relating to the verses of the Dhammapada and in the Poems of the Nuns (Theri Gatha).

Impermanence
'Whatever exists is without endurance. Hence the terms "flourishing" and "decaying".
A person is born and then dies. O! the happiness of freedom from this condition!

For a human life is like an earthen jar made in a potter's mill. Formed with care, all such are destined to destruction.'
                    (Tan-Poh and Fa-Kheu-King
                    – Chinese scriptures)

13 Buddhist art and architecture

This unit tells you how Buddhist art and architecture helps Buddhists to express, learn and live the Dhamma.

Interpreting the scriptures

Many Buddhists cannot read their scriptures because they do not know the language in which the scriptures are written or because their reading skills are poor. Instead, Buddhist art and architecture, along with oral teaching, allows them to learn the teaching and practise devotion and meditation. Buddhist art and architecture also enable Buddhists to express their reverence for the Buddha, Dhamma and the Sangha. Many Buddhists consider Buddhist art and architecture as important to their lives as the Buddhist scriptures.

Buddha images

At first the Buddha was represented by symbols such as a tree, a flower or a wheel. The first sculptures of the Buddha in human form date from the 1st century CE. Buddha images were made from wood, plaster and metal, and also carved from rock. The facial features often reflect those of the people in the country in which the image was made. The Buddha is shown in seated, standing, reclining or walking postures. The sculptures are expressions of the religious devotion of the artists. They are of different sizes. The images in the open air are often very big, while those inside temples and homes are smaller. The images reflect the Buddhist qualities of harmony, compassion, wisdom and tranquillity. Buddhist worship, which is a meditation on the Buddha, Dhamma and the Sangha, is normally facing a Buddha image. Mahayana and Vajrayana Buddhists have images of Buddhas like Amida and Mahavairochana, in addition to images of Sakyamuni Buddha, and of Bodhisattvas like Avalokitesvera, Manjusri and Tara.

Architecture

Emperor Asoka erected pillars in India with inscriptions from the Dhamma on them to make the teaching better known. The Sarnath pillar is well known because on top of it are statues of four lions facing in four directions, which have been adopted by India as its State emblem.

The Tissamaharama Dagoba, Sri Lanka.

A Shri Kalachakra Mandala from Tibet.

Buddhist monasteries and temples have decorative but dignified architecture. Temples were sometimes carved out inside huge rocks. There are well-known examples in India and Sri Lanka, and also the cave monastery of a Thousand Buddhas in China. In Japan Zen temples are simple, reflecting the character of Zen meditation.

Paintings

The walls and ceilings of temples often have paintings illustrating scenes from the **Jataka stories** and the Buddha's life. Some temples have life-size statues showing these scenes. Buddhists study these to learn and remember the Dhamma and associated stories.

In Japanese temples and monasteries there are beautiful paintings done in the Japanese style. Horyu-ji monastery has painted lacquer panels showing scenes from the Buddha's past lives (Jataka stories, *see* Unit 15) as well as other Buddhist paintings.

Stupas

A structure like the one shown in the photograph opposite is called a **stupa**, caitya, dagoba, pagoda, or chorten, depending on the country, and is usually a part of a temple complex. These structures are built to enshrine Buddhist relics and are objects of worship and meditation. The stupas differ in size and shape from country to country.

Different explanations are given as to what the various parts of the stupas represent. For instance , it is said that the ground on which the stupa stands represents **generosity**, the base represents moral restraint, the bell-shaped body the different worlds, and the spine Nibbana.

Tibetan art

In Tibet the Buddhists developed their own distinctive art. The most striking example is the **Mandala**. It is a picture of the Buddhist world of **deities** and beings, and at the same time, a map of a human being. A Mandala is used for meditation. There are also very brightly coloured paintings of Buddhas, Bodhisattas, deities and demons on monastery walls, and also on canvas, paper and silk hangings. In Japan the temples of certain traditions feature similar Mandalas.

NEW WORDS

Deities people born on a higher plane

Generosity considering and acting for the welfare of others

Jataka stories stories of the previous lives of the Buddha, used to illustrate Buddhist ethical ideas

Mandala a pictorial diagram of the world, and of a person, used for meditation

Stupa a circular structure containing Buddhist relics

Attaining the Buddha Way
'Those who worshipped relics
And built many sorts of stupas…
Or those who built stone shrines…
Or have erected images…
For the sake of Buddhas
Even children in their play who…
Have drawn Buddha's images,
All such ones as these…
Have attained the Buddha Way.'

(Lotus Sutra)

14 Moral values in the scriptures

The King of Hell orders wrong-doers to be punished by being plunged into boiling oil; life-size images at Buddhurajamaha Vihara, Dickwella, Sri Lanka.

This unit tells you about the essential moral values in Buddhism.

The moral values of Buddhism appear again and again in various parts of the scriptures. Living according to these moral values, **loving kindness**, compassion and respect for oneself and for others is the first stage of the Noble Eightfold Path (see Unit 9), and the foundation of a Buddhist life. These values are much the same in all schools and traditions of Buddhism.

Guidelines for living
The Five Precepts set out the essential guidelines for all Buddhists.
Not to:
1 harm other beings,
2 take what is not given,
3 misuse the senses,
4 speak in a way that is harmful to others and
5 take drugs or intoxicants which cloud the mind.

There are further Precepts to be observed on special occasions and more for monks and nuns. Tibetan Buddhism expresses the same ideas, calling them the Ten Non-Virtues (wrongful actions).

All these are expressed in negative ways but involve positive effort (see Unit 19). For example:

> 'Whosoever in this world destroys life, tells lies, takes what is not given, misuses the senses and is addicted to intoxicating drinks, such a one interferes with their own progress in this very world.'
>
> (The Dhammapada, v. 246 and 247)

In a book called the Sutra of the Forty-Two Chapters, which is thought to be the first Sutta translated into Chinese, the essential

Buddhist teachings were extracted from the various Suttas and set out as 42 paths. This Sutra says:

'The Buddha said, "For human beings, 10 things are evil. Three are of the body; four are of the mouth; and the other three are of the mind. The three (evils) of the body are needless killing, stealing and sensual misconduct. The four (evils) of the mouth are saying one thing but meaning another, slander, lying and improper language. The three (evils) of the mind are greediness, anger and foolishness."'

Livelihood and conduct

The Buddha explained the conditions of happiness in life as:

'Persistent effort, protecting one's earnings, good friendship, balanced livelihood, confidence in the Buddha, virtue, charity and wisdom.'   (Vyagghapajja Sutta)

'Right livelihood' is a part of the Noble Eightfold Path (see Unit 9) and means that one should avoid making a living directly or indirectly by a trade or profession which brings harm to others. Five kinds of trade are to be avoided – trading in arms and weapons, human beings, meat and fish, intoxicating drinks and substances, and poison.

The conditions which lead to a person's downfall are, for instance:

'1 keeping company with bad persons,
 2 being fond of sleep,
 3 not supporting one's parents,
 4 deceiving a holy man or teacher,
 5 being selfish,
 6 being conceited and looking down on others,
 7 being a drunkard or gambler,
 8 sexual misconduct,
 9 being angry,
10 not paying one's debts, and so on.'
                     (Parabhava and Vasala Suttas)

In India at the time of the Buddha, the Brahmins were understood to be the highest class (caste) of people. People inherited their caste from their parents. Other classes or castes had a lower status and the lowest were outcasts. However, the Buddha explained that a person should be judged by his or her actions and said:

'Not by birth is one an outcast,
Not by birth is one a Brahmin.
By deed one becomes an outcast,
By deed one becomes a Brahmin.'
                     (Vasala Sutta)

NEW WORD

Loving kindness affectionate consideration for others (metta)

Morality
'Who is tactful and energetic,
And gains wealth by his own effort;
He will acquire fame by truth,
And friendship by giving.

'He who has faith and is also truthful,
Virtuous, firm and fond of giving;
By virtue of these four conditions
Will never in the hereafter feel sorry.

'Truth and Restraint,
Charity and Forbearance,
Are the greatest reformers of human beings.'
                     (Alavaka Sutta)

This unit and the next tell you about the Jataka stories and relate two of these stories.

The Jakata stories are a collection of about 540 stories of the previous lives of Gotama Buddha, when he was born as a Bodhisatta, and his disciples. These stories are used to teach Buddhist moral values and are important because they illustrate Buddhist ideas like **Kamma** (Karma) and Rebecoming or Rebirth (see Unit 2), and Buddhist values like kindness and gratitude. Here is a typical and well-known story.

'The hunter and the monkeys

Once there lived in the Himalayan forests two monkeys who were brothers. The elder was called Nandiya. They headed a large band of monkeys and lived with their mother, who was elderly, frail and blind. They looked after their mother and brought food for her.

'One day, they went to another distant forest with the band of monkeys in search of food. The two brothers sent fruits and nuts to their mother by giving them to other monkeys to deliver. When they returned home they found that their mother was much

The hunter sees the monkeys.

weaker and thinner. She said that she had not received any of the food that they had sent her. The other monkeys had been eating the food.

'Nandiya decided that it was far more important to him to look after his mother than to rule the colony. He said to his brother, "You rule the colony, I shall take our mother to the distant forest and look after her." His brother replied, "I care not for ruling the colony. So I shall join you in looking after our mother." So the brothers led their mother to the distant forest and looked after her.

'In a nearby city there lived a man who had received a very good education from a famous teacher. When he had completed his education, the teacher, seeing that his pupil was a violent and cruel person, had said, "Do not do anything cruel which you will regret. People who are like you do not do well in life."

'Although he was educated, because of his nature, the man was not able to carry on in a suitable job. He had to earn a living as a hunter. He used to kill animals in the forest with his bow and arrow, sell the flesh and provide for his family.

'One day he came to the forest on a hunting trip and saw the three monkeys high up on a tree. At the same time the monkeys saw him. As he was preparing to use his bow and arrow Nandiya jumped in front of him and said, "Please do not kill my mother or brother. Instead, please kill me and sell my flesh." The hunter shot Nandiya and then prepared to shoot the mother. Then the brother jumped down and said, "Please do not kill my mother, kill me instead." The cruel hunter, without thinking about what he was doing, shot the brother and then the mother as well. He tied the dead monkeys together and carried them home.

'Before he reached home a thunderbolt struck his house, destroying it completely, and killing everyone in his family. When he reached home and saw what had happened he was overcome by grief.

'The Law of Kamma
He remembered his teacher's words not to do anything cruel which he might regret. "So this is what my teacher meant," the man thought, "Bad actions have bad consequences, good actions have good consequences."'

The Buddha, having related the story, explained the idea of rebirth by identifying the persons associated with him in his last life with the characters in the story. In this birth, Nandiya was Gotama Buddha; his brother was Ven. Ananda (see Unit 1); the famous teacher was Ven. Sariputta; and the cruel hunter was Ven. Devadatta. The mother monkey was Queen Prajapati Gotami, Prince Siddhatta's stepmother who looked after him when he was young (see Unit 8).

This story illustrates the Buddhist ideas of Kamma, Rebecoming or Rebirth and self-sacrifice, and the view that children, when grown up, should look after their elderly parents (see Unit 17).

The Jataka stories appear in the Sutta Pitaka of the Pali scriptures and also in the other scriptures.

NEW WORD

Kamma (Karma) the law that good actions and thoughts have good consequences and bad actions and thoughts have bad consequences

Kamma
'All beings are the owners of their deeds, the heirs of their deeds...and wherever the beings spring into existence, there their deeds will ripen.' (Anguttara Nikaya)

'If I had not done harm to others,
No harm would come to me;
If I did harm living beings –
It is fit that harm returns to me.'
(Bodhicaryavatara – Tibetan scriptures)

16 Vessantara Jataka

This unit tells the story of the previous life of the Bodhisatta before he was born as Prince Siddhattha (see Unit 1) to become Gotama Buddha. This story is often acted out in schools in Buddhist countries.

'Once upon a time there lived in India a King called Sandumaha who ruled the kingdom of Jayatura. The Bodhisatta was born as his son, Prince Vessantara. He grew up to be a very learned and kind person. The King entrusted the Prince with many duties of government which the Prince fulfilled to perfection.

'Many lives earlier, the Bodhisatta had decided to become a Buddha. During these lives he had developed his mind and the qualities necessary to realize his goal.

'Prince Vessantara practised generosity and charity, the greatest virtues. He helped his people and waged war against hunger, thirst, poverty, sickness and want. The people loved him. His fame spread beyond the kingdom. Jealous of the Prince's fame, a king in a neighbouring country sent some of his men to ask for the royal elephant on which the Prince used to ride. These men came dressed as holy men and asked for the elephant. Since he did not refuse any request for help the Prince gave the elephant to these men.

'King Sandumaha's Ministers were furious. They complained to the King and asked that the Prince be banished to the forest and made to feel sorry for this act. With a heavy heart, the King agreed to send his most senior Minister to tell the Prince of his decision. The Minister, with tears in his eyes, gave the message to the Prince. The Prince was surprised but accepted the decision. When he explained the position to his faithful wife Princess Mantridevi, she insisted on going too, along with their two small children, Krishnajina, a daughter, and Jalia, a son.

'The Prince gave away all his wealth to the people and the family went to live in a small

Prince Vessantara gives away his children;
life-size images at Buddhurajamaha Vihara, Dickwella, Sri Lanka.

hut in the forest. One day a wicked man, called Jujaka, came to their home. He said, "I have heard that you never refuse a request. I wish to ask for your two children to attend on my wife".

'The Prince was stunned and heartbroken. But because of his generous nature he granted the request. Because the Bodhisatta had developed the practice of **non-attachment** to a high level he was able to grant the man's request. At the same time, because of his love for his children and great compassion he wanted to ensure that they would be looked after by his father. So as the man took the children away, the Prince asked him to go and see his father King Sandumaha, who would pay money and get back the children. The Prince was confident that his father would do this.

'Princess Mantridevi had gone out to collect nuts and fruits. When she returned and heard why the children were not there she fainted. The Prince had to revive her by splashing water on her face. She too was heartbroken. The parents frequently offered prayers for the welfare of their children.

'Sakra, the chief of the deities, understood that Prince Vessantara was just one life away from becoming a Buddha and decided to test him. He came to the Prince in the form of a holy man and said, "I wish you to give your wife to me as a gift". The Prince and the Princess were dumbfounded. However, because of the generosity in his heart the Prince could not refuse and said that he would grant the request. Then, in admiration, Sakra said: "Only those whose hearts are purified can understand your actions. Because of your generosity and non-attachment you have given away your nearest and dearest. I am Sakra, the chief of the deities. I give back your good wife. Do not grieve over your children. Your father the King has got them back and will be here soon with them." He thought: "Surely the Bodhisatta is now near to Buddhahood. We all, the deities, human beings and all other beings bow before you in adoration."

'Having spoken to the Prince, Sakra disappeared and returned to his heavenly home. Not long after, King Sandumaha arrived, bringing the children with him. Prince Vessantara and his family returned to the palace with the King. The Ministers now understood the meaning of the Prince's actions and asked for forgiveness.'

Having related this story, the Buddha explained the meaning of rebirth by identifying the persons associated with him in his last life with the characters in the story and said,

'Princess Mantridevi was Yasodhara, Princess Krishnajina was Ven. Uppalavanna, Prince Jalia was Ven. Rahula and I was Prince Vessantara.'

This story illustrates the Buddhist virtues of generosity and charity, and the Buddhist ideas of non-attachment and Rebecoming or Rebirth.

NEW WORDS

Non-attachment not being attached to persons or things

Non-attachment
'For those who stand in the middle
of the water,
In the formidable stream,
For those who are overcome by decay
and death,
I will tell you of an island....

'This matchless island:
Possessing nothing and grasping
after nothing,
I call Nibbana, the destruction of decay and
death.'   (Sutta Nipata)

17 Human relationships and duties

This unit shows the respect with which the Buddha regarded family and social relations, and tells you about the duties attached to certain special human relationships, which are set out in the Sigalovada Sutta.

'Every morning a young man called Sigala used to worship the six geographical directions (north, east, south, west, overhead.and underfoot). One day the Buddha saw him and asked what he was doing. Sigala replied that just before dying his father had advised him to worship the six directions. "Look here, young man," the Buddha said, "Your father's advice is excellent, but the six directions are parents, teachers, wife and children, friends, employees and religious persons. These six groups should be worshipped because they are worthy of honour and respect. They are worshipped by performing one's duties towards them."

A cremation procession in Bali.

1 Parents and children

A child should:

  a support elderly parents,
  b perform duties to be done on their behalf,
  c maintain the family traditions,
  d be worthy of the parents and
  e perform the necessary funeral rites on their death.

A parent should:

  a guide the children away from bad conduct,
  b persuade them to lead good lives,
  c give them a good education,
  d advise them on marriage and
  e hand over any inheritance to them.

2 Teachers and pupils

A pupil should:

  a respect the teacher and be obedient,
  b attend on the teacher,
  c pay attention to the teaching,
  d do any work set by the teacher and
  e receive the teaching respectfully.

A teacher should:

  a teach suitable subjects,
  b see that the pupils understand what is taught,
  c instruct them in the arts and sciences,
  d give the pupils good references and
  e guide the pupils in later life.

3 Husband and wife

A husband should honour his wife, love her, be faithful to her, allow her to deal with the domestic matters and provide security and comfort.

A wife should perform her duties well, be hospitable to relatives, love and be faithful to her husband, manage the household finances and be skilled and energetic in her duties.

4 Friends, relatives and neighbours

One should be generous, courteous, helpful, impartial, sincere, loyal and not forsake them in times of difficulty and need.

5 Employers and employees

Employers should assign work according to ability, pay adequate wages and look after the employees. The employees, in turn, should perform their duties well and be loyal to the employer.

6 Religious persons

One should look after the material needs of religious and holy people and be willing to learn from them. In return a religious person should teach the religion to others, set an example of a good life and attend to the religious needs of others.'

You will see that the teaching of the Sigalovada Sutta ties up with the teaching in the Noble Eightfold Path (see Unit 9) and the teaching on moral values (see Unit 14). Harmonious and friendly family and social life is considered very important in Buddhism because it forms the basis of a stable society. In this Sutra the Buddha explained worship to mean being reverent, recognizing worthiness and paying respect.

Conditions of welfare

'Four conditions, Vyagghapajja, contribute to a person's welfare and happiness in this very life. Which four? The accomplishment of persistent effort, the accomplishment of watchfulness, good friendship and balanced livelihood.'

'Four conditions, Vyagghapajja, contribute to a persons welfare and happiness in the life to come. Which four? The accomplishment of faith, the accomplishment of virtue, the accomplishment of charity and the accomplishment of wisdom.'

(Vyagghapajja Sutta)

18 The Dhammapada

This unit tells you about the Dhammapada and its contents.

The Dhammapada is a collection of the most noteworthy sayings of the Buddha. Buddhists treasure and study them and try to live by them. Here are some of them:

General matters
A Introduction
'All **conditions** have mind as their originator; mind is their chief, and they are mind-made. If one speaks or acts with a wicked mind unhappiness follows him, even as the wheel follows the hoof of the draught-ox.'   (v.1)

'Similarly, if one speaks or acts with a pure mind, happiness follows him like a shadow that never leaves.'   (v.2)

'In those who harbour such thoughts as: he abused me, he struck me, he overcame me, he robbed me – hatred never ceases.'   (v.3)

'In those who do not harbour such thoughts hatred will cease.'   (v.4)

'Hatreds never cease by hatred in this world. Through kindness alone they cease. This is an ancient law.'   (v.5)

B Foolishness
'A fool who thinks he is a fool is for that reason a wise man: the fool who thinks that he is wise is called a fool indeed.'   (v.63)

'Green Khadiravani Tara', a Mandala from Tibet.

C Wisdom

'As a solid rock is not shaken by the wind, even so the wise are not shaken by praise or blame.' (v.81)

'Self-conquest is, indeed, far better than the conquest of all other folk.' (v.104)

Personal matters
D Punishment

'All tremble at punishment. Life is dear to all: comparing others with **oneself**, one should neither kill nor cause to kill.' (v.130)

E The self

'One is the guardian of oneself; what other guardian could there be? With oneself fully controlled, one obtains a protector who is hard to obtain.' (v.160)

'By oneself is evil done, by oneself is one defiled. By oneself is one purified. Purity and impurity depend on oneself. No one can purify another.' (v.165)

F Happiness

'Victory breeds hatred; the defeated live in pain. The peaceful ones live happily, giving up victory and defeat.' (v.201)

G Anger

'One should give up anger; one should abandon pride.' (v.221)

'Conquer anger by kindness; conquer evil by good; conquer the stingy by giving; conquer the liar by truth.' (v.223)

H Handicaps

'Whosoever in this world destroys life, tells lies, takes what is not given, misuses the senses and is addicted to intoxicating drinks, such a one interferes with their own progress in this very world.'

(v.246 and 247)

I Miscellaneous

'If by giving up a slight happiness one may achieve a larger one, let the wise person give up the lesser happiness in consideration for the greater happiness.' (v.290)

'He who wishes his own happiness by causing pain to others is not released from hatred, being himself entangled in the tangles of hatred.' (v.291)

J The wise man

'He that does no evil through body, speech or mind, who is restrained in these three respects, him I call a wise man.' (v.391)

The Dhammapada was arranged and classified in its present form at the First Council and is a part of the Buddhist scriptures. It consists of about 420 verses, arranged in 26 chapters, and each verse is accompanied by a story about the persons and circumstances related to the saying.

Karma (Kamma)

'If it's suffering you fear, if it's suffering you dislike,
Do no evil deeds at all – for all to see or secretly.

'Not in the sky nor in the ocean's middle,
Nor if you were to hide in cracks in the mountains,
Can there be found on this wide earth a corner
Where karma does not catch up with the culprit.' (Sanskrit Dharmapada)

NEW WORDS

Condition a mental or physical thing or state

Oneself the person; though Buddhism teaches that there is no self, the person is recognized for practical purposes

Buddhists worshipping at the Kelaniya temple in Sri Lanka.

This unit tells you how the scriptures are used in devotion and worship in the Theravada countries like Burma, Cambodia, Laos, Sri Lanka and Thailand.

Paying homage to The Triple Gem

Devotion and worship are an important part of Buddhist life. Worship is not an empty ritual but is a meaningful act accompanied by knowledge and **mindfulness**. Theravada Buddhism considers the Buddha to have been an extraordinary person who has passed away. Therefore worship is not a communication with the Buddha but rather a reflection or meditation on his life and the Dhamma, and a reminder to live according to the teaching.

Gotama Buddha said:

'Whoever, a monk, nun or lay person, lives in accordance with the teaching, conducts himself or herself dutifully and acts correctly, he or she respects, honours, worships and venerates the Buddha with the highest kind of worship.'   (Maha Parinibbana Sutta)

Devotional activities may be in the temple or at home, on festival days, full-moon days, special occasions or daily, and are performed facing a Buddha image.

After paying homage to the Buddha, the lay person recites, or if a monk is conducting the worship follows the monk in reciting, the Three Refuges:

'I take Refuge in the Buddha.

I take Refuge in the Dhamma.

I take Refuge in the Sangha.'

This is recited three times. Offerings of

flowers, lamps and incense are made with the recitation of certain phrases. Then, verses in praise of the Triple Gem, the Buddha, the Dhamma and the Sangha, are recited.

Next, for both general worship and special occasions, it is usual to recite certain scriptures. The most common Suttas are the Mangala Sutta, Karaniya Metta Sutta and the Ratana Sutta. This recitation is the chanting or Pirit (see Unit 3).

Devotion on the blessings of life

In the Mangala Sutta the Buddha explains the **blessings** of life as:

> '1 Not to associate with fools, but to associate with the wise, to honour those who are worthy of honour.
> 2 To reside in a suitable locality, to have done worthy actions and to set oneself on the right course.
> 3 Much learning, good livelihood, highly trained discipline, pleasant speech.
> 4 Support of parents, cherishing the family.
> 5 Generosity.
> 6 Avoiding unskilful actions, and intoxicants.
> 7 Reverence, humility, contentment, gratitude.
> 8 Patience, obedience, religious discussion.
> 9 Self-control, understanding the Dhamma.
> 10 Having a steady mind.'

These are all factors which, according to the scriptures, contribute to a good Buddhist life.

Devotion on loving kindness

The Buddha explains the standard of moral conduct required of a Buddhist and the way to practise loving kindness.

> 'He should make the right effort, be skilled in living, honest, obedient, gentle, humble, contented, with few requirements for life, have a simple livelihood, control the senses,

be prudent, courteous and not seek constant company (be happy in his or her own company).' (Karaniya Metta Sutta, Teaching on Loving Kindness)

The cultivation of loving kindness and compassion to all beings is an important part of Buddhist practice.

> The Buddha advises his followers, 'Not to do wrong, not to deceive or despise another, not to wish any harm to another, to have compassion for all beings as a mother loves her children, to develop mindfulness, not to have wrong views, to be virtuous and endowed with insight, and not to be attached to sensual pleasures.' (Karaniya Metta Sutta)

The Buddha urged his followers to show loving kindness even to those who are hostile, and explained the importance of the teachings in the Ratana Sutta.

NEW WORDS

Blessings good fortune, wish for good fortune
Mindfulness concentration

Worship – Buddha, Dhamma, Sangha
'The Buddhas of the ages past,
The Buddhas that are yet to come,
The Buddhas of the present age,

'The Dhammas of the ages past,
The Dhammas that are yet to come,
The Dhammas of the present age,

'The Sanghas of the ages past,
The Sanghas that are yet to come,
The Sanghas of the present age,
Humbly I worship you.'
                    (From Theravada worship)

This unit tells you how the scriptures are used in devotion and worship in Japan and Tibet.

Devotion in Japan

Throughout Japan daily services are held in Buddhist temples. They are conducted by resident priests who chant the Suttas and **mantras** revered by the particular tradition. On festival days there are special programmes.

Buddhists usually have a shrine at home called a Butsudan. It will have an image of Sakyamuni Buddha, or another Buddha or a Bodhisatta of Mahayana Buddhism, Sutra texts and ancestral mortuary tablets dedicated to deceased relatives. The family worship here regularly, perhaps every day.

The Sutras chanted depend on the tradition. The Lotus Sutra is highly revered particularly in the Tendai, Soto-Zen and Nichiren sects. Other generally popular Sutras are the Heart Sutra and the Wisdom Sutra. A popular chant is Chapter 25 of the Lotus Sutra which has these words:

A Tendai priest worshipping at a shrine in his home in England.

'Bodhisattva Avalokitesvara, pure and holy,
In pain, distress, death, calamity,
Able to be a sure reliance,
Perfect in all merit,
With compassionate eyes beholding all,
Boundless ocean of blessings!
Prostrate let us revere him.'   (Lotus Sutra)

Devotion in Tibet

In Tibet the scriptures are recited at the services and worship held in the temples and monasteries daily and on festival days. Individual devotions are performed morning and evening at the private shrines at home. Books are considered to be more sacred than images as they contain the teaching. These devotions include readings from the scriptures.

The Tibetan Scriptures refer to mantras. These are words or phrases which monks and lay people keep repeating in order to progress spiritually. The mantra of Bodhisattva Avalokatisvara, 'Om Mani Padme Hum' ('Hail the Jewel in the Lotus') is chanted frequently. Mantras are sometimes written down and placed in prayer wheels after being **consecrated** by rituals performed by Lamas. Sometimes they are carved on the prayer wheel and then consecrated. Turning the wheel mindfully brings the same benefit as reciting the mantra.

Tibetan scriptures refer to the special dance ceremonies not found in any other Buddhist tradition. The dancers wear masks and elaborate costumes, and act out sacred historical stories. These dances are performed at monastic festivals and are a moving and powerful emotional, devotional and spiritual experience for both dancers and spectators.

Rev. Daishin Morgan of the Order of Buddhist Contemplatives writes:

'I love to go to ceremonies and festivals because they express what I feel in my heart in a way that goes beyond words and touches the emotions. The more I have learned of meditation (see Unit 21), the more I find that there is a peacefulness inside me within which joy and gratitude can arise. The ceremonies express this and help me to explore this side of myself. I find it a joy to join with others in an expression of gratitude for the teaching. Ceremonies and festivals are also an active form of meditation, they are means of showing how simple actions can have deep meaning.'

Ganshin Rock, a Tendai priest, writes:

'The form of worship can vary from meditation upon one's own temporary existence and continual change to the chanting of mantras and performing ceremonies dedicated to specific Buddhas or Bodhisattas.

The study and chanting of Buddhist Sutras (scriptures) and the recitation of mantras (mystic formulas) are all recognized ways of worship in Buddhism. However, as a priest of a Mahayana tradition, for me the most essential things is to follow the Four Noble Truths and Noble Eightfold Path, and to bear in mind that I am a part of the great universal life force present in every living being and should therefore devote my energies with wisdom and compassion.'

NEW WORDS

Consecrated dedicated in a religious way
Mantra set of words having a religious significance

Devotion in Tibet

'Do not despise your own or other's religion
Show pure loving-kindness toward all living beings…
Do not abuse the life energies of yourself or others.
Do not trouble the existence of worldly people.

'It is also wrong to despise
The wisdom nature of women.'

(Krsnayamari Tantra)

21 Meditation

This unit tells you what the scriptures say about meditation. Meditation is taught on a personal basis and is best done under guidance.

Understanding and living the teaching

The Buddhist scriptures enable a Buddhist not just to understand the teaching but actually to live it. The Noble Eightfold Path gives guidance to a person on how to live a good life. The first stage is to develop morality and inner discipline, and the second stage is meditation or mental culture. These need to be developed together. Certain aspects of Buddhism cannot be taught, learned or understood intellectually. They need to be experienced by meditation.

The word 'meditation' is a poor translation of the Pali word 'Bhavana', which means the cultivation and development of the mind. This includes the more formal sitting and walking meditation, and also informal meditation – awareness and mindfulness during all daily activities.

Different aspects of meditation

All meditation starts with mindfulness of breathing. There are two parts to meditation. The first (Samatha) leads to tranquillity. This involves concentration on subjects such as a colour, the virtues of the Buddha, compassion and so on. The second (Vipassana) meditation involves concentration on elements of Buddhist teaching like impermanence and dukkha. This leads to seeing things as they really are and to Nibbana or Enlightenment.

The Buddha said:

'Two things are conducive to knowledge: tranquillity and insight. When tranquillity is developed mind is developed. When insight is developed right understanding is developed.'
(Anguttara Nikaya)

The most important discourse given by the Buddha on meditation is the Satipatthana Sutta, where the Buddha says:

'This is the unique way for the purification of beings, for the destruction of suffering, for the attainment of wisdom and for the realization of Nibbana – namely the Four Foundations of Mindfulness.

Herein a disciple lives:

1 contemplating the body
2 contemplating the feelings
3 contemplating the states of mind
4 contemplating the Dhammas
   (the contents of thoughts).'

This Sutta explains the practice of concentration on the 'in-and-out-breathing' which is one of the most common and popular forms of meditation. It also explains another very important meditation

A monk meditating at the Dodanduwa temple in Sri Lanka.

Young monks meditating at Fayuan temple in Beijing in China.

which is to be mindful of everything one says and does all the time. In fact, Buddhist worship is a form of meditation (see Unit 19).

Some different types of meditation

Zen Buddhism in Japan uses **Koans** – riddles which have no meaning and are designed to take the mind to a high spiritual level in meditation. For example:

'You know the sound of two hands clapping,

What is the sound of one hand clapping?'

Tibetan Buddhism uses the Mandala as an aid to meditation.

Ven. Myokyo-ni, a senior nun ordained in the Zen tradition writes:

'Usually, clear awareness is clouded by our thoughts, wishes, fears, opinions, anger, etc. Meditation uncovers this awareness, as when the sun breaks through clouds.

So in the practice of meditation we learn to forget ourself and to become unselfish and kind-hearted, that is, happy and considerate of each other, gladly lending a helping hand when required.'

Mrs. Ruki Shillam, a Sri Lankan Buddhist writes:

'It is only during meditation that the mind could be watched and reflected upon. By developing this practice, the importance given to thinking is diminished and life becomes simpler. Things can be seen and understood more clearly.'

NEW WORD

Koan riddle used for meditation in Zen Buddhism

Mindfulness

'While going, standing, sitting, or lying down, the disciple understands the expressions; "I go", "I stand", "I sit", "I lie down".

'The disciple acts with clear mindfulness in going and coming; in looking forward and back; in bending and stretching... in eating, drinking, chewing and tasting... in walking, standing, sitting, falling asleep, awakening... in speaking and keeping silent.'

(Satipatthana Sutta)

This unit gives you the opinions of a variety of people on what the Buddhist scriptures mean to them.

a Rev. Phoebe Van Woerden, a nun ordained in the Order of Buddhist Contemplatives:

'The Buddhist scriptures are to me the voices of good and wise friends, who have walked the path of meditation before. They give clear instructions for meditation and training, and they encourage me when the going is hard. They console me when I am sad or worried, and help me to keep a bright heart. They explain the meaning of life and death, as they really are, so that I can come to understand my own purpose in this life more and more deeply. Then, when in my meditation there arises compassion and understanding, the scriptures will confirm that and rejoice with me.'

b Bhikkhu Seevali, a Nepalese monk ordained in the Theravada tradition:

'These scriptures are sacred for me and spiritually valuable. The Pali canon consists of Buddhist texts which are the Buddha's word delivered for the well-being of the many. These teachings are based on the practice and experience he went through. So we, too, as his followers, can follow that path. The scriptures are rich in moral and spiritual value.'

A monk meditating at the Chithurst Forest Monastery in England.